101 T
Dad Never Told
You About Men

The Good, Bad, and Ugly Things
Men Want and Think About Women
and Relationships

By Bruce Bryans

Legal Disclaimer

Although the information in this book may be very useful, it is sold with the understanding that neither the author nor the publisher is engaged in presenting specific psychological, emotional, or sexual advice. Nor is anything in this book intended to be a diagnosis, prescription, recommendation, or cure for any specific kind of psychological, emotional, or sexual problem. Each person has unique needs and this book cannot take these individual differences into account.

ISBN-13: 978-1507821756

ISBN-10: 1507821751

My Free Gift to You

As a way of saying "thanks" for your purchase, I'm offering a free 10-lesson email course (and other assorted goodies) that are exclusive to my book readers. Each lesson reveals some of my best-kept dating secrets for cultivating **long-term attraction** with high-quality men.

You can access it at:

http://www.brucebryans.com/ecourse/

In this free course, you will not only learn the most high-value dating behaviors that make men burn with desire and desperate to commit to a woman, but you'll also learn how to confidently interact with men so that you can get the guy you want, keep him interested, and quickly weed out time-wasters, players, and men who'll never commit.

Again, you can access it at:

http://www.brucebryans.com/ecourse/

Table of Contents

Introduction

Let's face it; there's only so much that your good old Dad (assuming he was around) could have done to keep you well-informed about how men think and what we want when it comes to love, sex, and romance. Many women aren't fortunate enough to have good father figures in their lives, and even those that did probably still weren't told the full secrets about what makes men tick.

This book, *101 Things Your Dad Never Told You About Men*, is going to fill in the gaps of knowledge where your Dad might have failed to do so. Maybe the topic of how to please your husband in bed would have been too awkward a conversation, or perhaps talking about the emotional needs of a man was beyond his comfort level to share. Whatever the reason, your good old Dad probably never told you the ugly truth about what men want from women. But today we're going to fix that.

If you feel powerless when it comes to dating and relating to men, then you probably just don't understand what it is that a good man really wants from a woman. Notice that I didn't simply use the word "man" but I'm actually referring specifically to "a good man." You know, the type of guys that make phenomenal boyfriends and spectacular husbands.

As you go through this book I want you to keep this distinction in mind. There is a BIG difference between the average Joe and what many women perceive to be Mr. Right. No two guys are going to be exactly alike and no two guys are going to want the same thing from women. However, there are certain things that all high-quality men *prefer* when it comes to dating and relating to women. This is the distinction that I want to make, simply because no two guys will want the same thing (or the same woman) and no two women will want the same thing.

The problem I see with a lot of relationship advice books is that they give general advice to women about understanding men. The purpose of this book is to help women to understand not just any man, but high-quality, mature, masculine men. These are the men that prefer to be with high-quality, mature, feminine women. These are the men that prefer a passionate, fun, committed relationship with a phenomenal woman instead of a one-night-stand.

So if you're interested in these kinds of men this book is going to be of immense value to you. And whether you're currently dating or trying to find Mr. Right, this book will help you to get into the minds of these kinds of men so that you can figure out exactly what they are thinking. Even if you're already in a serious relationship the insights presented in this book still apply. You'll have an insider's look into what high-quality men want and think about when it comes to women and relationships. But most importantly, this book will show you how to *influence* the man of your dreams because you'll know exactly what makes him tick.

Now, there's one thing you must do as you read through this book. You must keep in mind that the advice within was written for women, not men. If some of the points seem to be a bit one-sided that's because I'm focusing on what you, as a woman, bring to the table when it comes to dating and relating with men. In the books I write for guys, I provide them with the ugly truth as well so that they'll "man up" and do what's necessary to become the kind of men that a good woman wants, needs, and deserves in her life. I pull no punches in the books I write for guys and I won't do so with you either. So keep that in mind as you discover all the good, bad, and ugly things men want and think about women and relationships.

It is <u>Imperative</u> That You Understand Your Man

Being a guy, I can honestly tell you this one simple fact about us: More than anything we want to be understood on a deep, deep level by ONE woman, and we want her to respect, love, desire, and support us because of that deep understanding. And when we find that woman, we want to give her more than ourselves; we want to give her the world.

Most guys will not admit that to a woman, and even more have no idea that's what they really want. The mature man realizes that his happiness AND true success in life is intrinsically linked to finding the right woman and loving her with all that he has to offer. Smart women also realize that their happiness in life is directly linked to their ability to find the right man, get him to commit, and make him happy.

So therein lies our problem. How can a woman find the right man (a quality man) and keep him happy if she

3

doesn't know what's going on in his head? Why should a man give you his heart and the world if he feels as if you just don't "get him"? Remember, he wants to be understood just as much as you do, maybe even more so, but men these days just don't know how to communicate their deepest needs in an honest, healthy way, especially to women.

Most men tend to develop along these lines:

As the young male develops, he starts out as a vulnerable little boy and needs the nurturing of his mother to help him grow. If he's lucky, he also has his father in his life guiding and teaching him in the way a young boy should act.

And keep in mind that a lot of guys don't have very emotionally open relationships with their fathers. But that's a subject for another day. But I want you to think of his heart at this point like a castle, and the doors to this castle are swung wide open where anything can enter as he is exposed to his environment.

Then as he grows and he becomes more exposed to the outside world, reality hits and soon circumstances teaches him that he must keep that door closed as much as possible. He soon learns that men need to be strong; he learns that he shouldn't cry, or maybe a bad experience with a woman completely changes his view of intimacy with women. He becomes less open about the way he feels and conceals his true emotions either to appear strong or to avoid pain. In any case, because of this he closes the doors shut and becomes more cautious to who and what he allows to enter. He feels secure and in control of his emotions, which gives him a deep sense of satisfaction as a man.

But then he meets a great woman. Someone he can depend and rely on, and someone with whom he can put his trust in…completely. But deep down inside he knows that in order to give himself to this woman he must open up those doors. In order for him to truly love her and allow her to enjoy the gift of loving him, he must open up the doors to his heart and give her the keys. But he's terrified of what she may find within him, and he doubts if she can respect, love, and support him if he reveals his vulnerabilities to her. A part of him wants to open those doors, but in reality he just doesn't know how. Sadly, a lot of guys aren't equipped or prepared to do this. In fact, a lot of great guys out there simply do not know HOW to do this.

Past experiences have taught them that to be so vulnerable as a man is suicide and ridiculous. For a woman, it may be romantic and show her that he truly loves her, but for a man it may be extremely awkward and uncomfortable. Because of this, many men are in fact incapable of opening those doors themselves, unless the right woman comes along who has the keys.

So what's a girl to do then? Well, first you're going to have to learn how to understand him, and secondly, you need to use that understanding to get him to open up emotionally. Why? Because the key to making a man fall in love and STAY in love with you lies in your ability to connect with him on a deep, emotional level. You need to connect with his heart before he can completely commit himself to you.

Truth is, every mature man knows that being influenced by the right woman can and will make him a better man, but you can only influence a man when his heart is open to that influence. Meet his deepest needs, no matter how good, bad, or ugly they are, and he will fight to win you and keep you in his life as long as he has breath in him. That's a promise.

Anyway, that's enough of my rambling. Let's dive into the minds of men, shall we?

<u>Chapter 1:</u>

Giving Him What He Needs

1

Men need respect the way women need love.

If you cannot respect a man through the way you communicate and act with him, then it will be impossible for him to fall in love or stay in love with you. A man can appreciate a woman's love only after his need for her respect and admiration has been met. Give a man your respect and admiration (focus on the things about him you esteem highly) and he will do whatever he can to keep you around...for good.

2

He needs appreciation too. Always consider and appreciate how hard he works to be a good man.

Most men secretly crave appreciation, but they'll never admit it for fear of looking needy or weak. Nobody is perfect, sweetheart, so if you take the time to notice, chances are he's doing a lot more to make you happy than you realize. The more you appreciate a man, I mean REALLY appreciate him, the better he'll feel about himself. The better he feels about himself the more confident he'll be in his ability to love you, romance you, and make you happy.

Whenever you genuinely appreciate a man his value both to himself and to you greatly increases. If you want to make a man feel good about himself tell him all of the things you love about him, but be authentic. A man loves it when a woman can give him *authentic appreciation.* Paying him a compliment that he knows isn't genuine will only make him feel as if you're trying to sweet talk him.

3

Be genuinely interested and supportive of his work or his passion. A man's self esteem is intrinsically tied to his life's purpose.

The work a man does is just as important to him as who he decides to spend his life with. A man's purpose and the woman he chooses to support him in achieving that purpose are intrinsically linked and account for most of his happiness and well-being. So if you're looking for Mr. Right, find a man whose life's purpose you can support wholeheartedly.

The future bliss of your relationship partly depends on your ability to support and respect his work. If you've already found your dream guy, ensure that you communicate to him your admiration for what he does or what he desires to someday do. Always encourage him to pursue the things that bring him a sense of joy and fulfillment.

4

Don't be upset if your man doesn't want to spend his every waking moment with you. He needs time to unwind and not worry about being a paragon of masculine perfection.

Some men need more space than others. The important thing is to know yourself and know what you're willing to compromise with. Being artistic and creative in nature, I tend to crave extended periods of solitude and reflection to be inspired to create. Some women can handle that, others probably cannot. Ensure that you know how much space a man requires for his emotional well-being. Understand his needs and allow him to be authentic with you without taking things personally. Sometimes a man just needs some time to himself.

5

Pay close attention to his needs. They are not the same as yours.

A man's needs are not only unique because of his gender but also because of his personality. Don't think that just because you have a certain need he has that need as well. Women who can attract and keep a good man all have at least one thing in common...they know how to cater to a man's unique needs.

Have you ever heard a happy and very much in love man say this about his woman - "She just gets me." This is a man who has found a woman that truly understands what he's all about. ALL men want this, and they'll give the world to the woman that can make them feel this way.

6

Guy time is a necessity. Give him the space he needs to spend time with his buddies.

Men need to be surrounded by other men not only for fun and friendship but also because it's important for their psychological and emotional development as men. As iron sharpens iron, a man literally becomes the company he keeps. Assuming that his friends are a good influence on him, give him the time he needs with his buddies to ensure that his masculine energies are renewed. And once his masculine energies have been renewed, he can be the man you need him to be and more.

7

Every man needs to feel needed by the woman he loves and adores.

The fastest way to lose a man is to make him feel as if you don't need him in your life. Let me be blunt, a man NEEDS to feel NEEDED by a woman before he can fall in love with her. And one of the ways to keep a man around for the long-term is to continue to do whatever you can to make him *feel* needed. There's nothing wrong with playing the damsel in distress every now and then to keep him interested, right?

8

Sex and a good home-cooked meal will not be enough to keep your husband happy or at home.

There's a false idea in society that says that all men need is sex and a good home-cooked meal to stay committed and interested in a relationship. If this were the case then all female prostitutes and chefs would make the most stellar partners, right? Wrong.

Men require a deep emotional connection that transcends his most basic, primal needs. Even beyond emotional chemistry, a man needs emotional support from his wife. Find out what his aspirations are and help him to succeed in whatever he does. A *very* supportive wife is a priceless find in today's world.

14

Chapter 2:

What Makes Him Tick

9

Men thrive more easily in relationships that foster their need to lead. Allow him the opportunity to do so, often.

Allowing a man to lead has nothing to do with you becoming his slave or minion. The more you encourage a man to take responsibility and make decisions the more confident he will become as a man. The added benefit is that he'll see you as his right-hand mate and number one confidant. Gently (and gracefully) encourage him to make decisions, and let him know that you trust (and respect) his judgment.

10

Every man has an inner child. This is a good thing.

Men need to play and recreate just like anyone else. Always give a man the room he needs to be himself and allow him to express his inner child without judgment. As we mature as men, there are many things that we stop doing because those habits and activities simply do nothing to make us better men. However, you'll find that we still maintain a certain inner boyishness that keeps us curious about the world and makes us a blast to be around.

11

Men don't really like guessing games. So hinting isn't the best strategy. Be honest but kind when communicating your needs.

Unless you've been with a man for years and he knows you in and out, subtle hints don't work with most guys. Men aren't fixated on figuring women out as much as women are about trying to figure them out. Guys just want to know how to make you happy and keep you that way. Simple. Let him know what makes you happy and what doesn't, but be classy about it. A good man always respects and appreciates a woman's honesty.

12

Men are visual creatures. He will notice other women. A good man will stop at just noticing.

Don't hate your man if you catch him looking at an attractive woman. Of course, you are free to *graciously* voice your displeasure if you catch him ogling other women. Men are naturally designed to assess a woman's beauty. It is instinctual for a man to look and appreciate, but it takes split-second decision-making for him to divert his eyes and move on. A good man will train himself to make that decision consistently.

13

If you go to a man with a problem, he will probably try to fix it. If you don't want him to fix it, let him know beforehand.

If you have a problem and you just want your man to listen to you, sometimes it helps to let him know that beforehand. Remember, be authentic and tell him that you'd like it if he just listens to you without him trying to problem solve. We can be highly logical creatures, and pussyfooting around a problem just doesn't make sense for most guys. In a man's mind, problems are not meant to be discussed until we feel better about ourselves…they are meant to be solved.

14

Men are naturally hard-wired to pursue women. Just because he's caught you doesn't mean the game should end.

Getting your current guy to be a little more interested in you requires the fine art of seduction; the good kind of seduction. If you want a man's preoccupation to be you, you'll need to step your game up and give him a reason to take notice. Trust me, if you go the extra mile to get his attention he'll be happy to follow your lead when you take the initiative to sparks things up.

15

Contrary to popular belief, your children should never take the place of your husband. Husband first, children second.

I don't know where this whole idea came from, but thinking that your husband should come second to your children is ludicrous. Now, I'm not saying that a child should be ignored until Daddy's needs are met. All I'm saying is that prioritizing the needs of the man you married is essential to the wellbeing of your marriage. No husband wants to feel as if his child is more important or essential to your happiness than he is.

16

Men are highly logical creatures. If he can get all the sex he can get without a full commitment...he's going to try to get all the sex he can get without a full commitment.

You know the old saying... "Why buy the cow when

the milk is already free?" That's exactly how it is with men and sexual conquest. No commitment should be based on the sex alone, but if YOU want a true commitment and he's getting what he wants (sex), then why should he give you what you want? To him, it's simply illogical.

17

A grown-up boy is a lot of fun to date but lacks true substance when it comes to relationships. He'll do whatever he can to have his way with you.

A *man* will use his boyish charms to get your attention, but he'll display his character to keep your attention. A *boy* will use his boyish charms to get your attention, to keep your attention, and to distract you from his immaturity. A grown-up *boy* is usually selfish and will take more than he gives. A mature *man* gives of himself for the joy of giving. Learn the difference in the guys you come across.

18

If a man is interested in you, he WILL try to impress you. Some men are just better at hiding it.

Be on the lookout for things such as playful teasing, boasting, acting nonchalant/aloof, paying extra attention to his appearance, and even gentlemanly gestures. A man will go the extra mile to impress a woman. He will always try to put his best foot forward and focus on his strengths to attract the woman he wants. Take nothing for granted and observe him carefully to see if he is going out of his way to get your attention.

19

Even a good man may lie to keep you from freaking out. Men will say anything to keep a woman's emotions on the level.

It's not that a woman's emotions are terrifying; it's just that they can *appear* wild, random, and uncontrollable in the eyes of men. When a man learns a woman's moods and what can trigger a negative emotional response, he may opt for the *easy* way out by telling a little white lie. I'm referring to simple things in this case such as forgetting to call or not taking out the trash. If he's not in the mood to be a big man and deal with your emotions...he'll tell you what you *need* to hear to keep things running smoothly.

20

Men tend to act like children when they are sick. Treat them tenderly during this more vulnerable time.

If he's feeling sick and he knows (albeit subconsciously) that he can gain a little bit more tender, love, and care from his woman, a man may act just a little more helpless than he really is. All he really wants is some sympathy and the nurturing attention of the woman he loves. To him, it's an excuse to be served hand and foot.

21

**A man wants his woman to be deeply
interested in something about him. If he
has a hobby or passion, find ways to make
it more enjoyable for him.**

If your man has a hobby he's passionate about, find
ways to make it even more enjoyable for him. If he has a
talent that he enjoys developing, do whatever you can to
ensure that he reaches his full potential. Anything that
gives him a sense of enjoyment (and is constructive in
some way) is good for his psychological well-being.
Either find a way to become interested in it with him or
find a way to add to his enjoyment.

22

**Never tempt a man to do anything you
really don't want him to do.**

No matter how angry you think you are or how
emotional you might be, it is ALWAYS a bad idea to

challenge a man to do something that you really don't want him to do. Now, most men are reasonable and understanding enough to know when you're not in your right mind (yes, I said it), but there will be times when he may not be in his right mind either. Refrain from challenging or tempting a man into doing something that you might regret later on.

23

Men love women that dress sexy and lust for women that dress slutty. There is a difference.

Men are highly visual creatures, and they make snap judgments about a woman based on what she communicates through her appearance. Dressing in a sexy way simply means catching his attention and engaging his *romantic* imagination. You will be seen as something worth pursuing because of your modest beauty and alluring mystery. Dressing slutty will grab his attention and overload the primal parts of his imagination. You will be perceived as a sex object worth getting into bed as quickly as humanly possible.

24

Men love to show their woman off to the world. Don't give him a reason to be ashamed of having you on his arm.

A good man wants a queen on his arm. He's not necessarily looking for eye candy, but what he does want is a woman that makes him want to say, "She's all mine!" Don't give a man any reason to hesitate showing you off to the world. If he's reluctant to introduce you to friends and family as his one-and-only, you might want to ask yourself why. If he's hesitant to take you out with him during social engagements you might want to figure out what's wrong. If a man is really interested in you and *proud* to be with you, he'll WANT to show you off.

Chapter 3:

Do's – The Secrets to Making Him Happy

25

Sometimes a man may fall in love with you because you listen to him.

The skill of active listening is not common. Therefore, a woman who has the ability to listen to a man with deep empathy will be rewarded with his undying loyalty. When a man talks to you, focus not only on what he's saying, but also on what he's trying to communicate. Learn how to quiet your mind and give him your full attention. This will communicate to him that you actually understand him. The better you become at listening to him, the more you will understand a man. A man will treasure the woman that truly "gets" him.

26

Make him feel like the king of his castle and he'll be more inclined to treat you like the queen.

In this world we all have to give in order to receive. So, when it comes to the home, treat your man like the king and he will gladly return the favor. Ensure that your home is a place of peace and harmony. Do whatever is necessary to keep conflicts and quarrels outside of the bedroom. Cater to his most basic needs without complaint and do so for the joy of serving him. A good man will undoubtedly take notice and do whatever he can to ensure that his queen is treated like royalty as well.

27

Support and encourage his goals. This will help to make you invaluable to him.

The woman who helps her man succeed is worth more than a fortune. If she becomes an integral part of her man's achievements she will gain a good man's undying loyalty and commitment. A good man wants his woman to be irreplaceable and indispensable to him. If a man feels as if he can succeed *better* in life without you...your chances of sustaining his long-term interests are next to zero.

28

Men require space and silence to fuel their romantic desire. Knowing when to withdraw your attention and conversation will make you irresistible to the man you love and want.

A woman who knows when to withdraw her attention in order to give a man a little space and silence is extremely attractive. The art of selective silence and becoming engrossed in your own concerns gives a man both the mental and physical space he needs to miss you. Your silence and lack of attention can create a lot of room for a man to desire more intimacy with you, especially if he's become overly accustomed to your presence and conversation.

29

A good man will do many things for you that he doesn't enjoy doing. Take notice of

the things he does and show him your

appreciation in any way you can.

He'll do things for you because he loves you and wants to make you happy. He'll also do things for you because he'd rather not deal with being nagged or bullied emotionally. If you want a man to do nice things for you of his own accord, figure out what makes him feel appreciated and do those things.

30

When the rest of your friends are

discussing all the negative things about

their boyfriends or husbands, praise your

man instead.

When your girlfriends are man-bashing or even just expressing their on-going discontent with their husbands or boyfriends, choose the higher road and talk positively about your man. Don't fall into the trap of thinking negatively about your man; it's not healthy for your relationship. Besides, any man would rather you praised him for his strengths as opposed to glorifying his weaknesses, even if he isn't around to hear it.

31

Men love being served their favorite things by their favorite girl.

After a long, hard days work, nothing says, "I love you" like a big tall glass of his favorite beverage. If you can do this with a pleasant attitude it's much easier for him to relax and act more lovingly towards you. It doesn't have to be a drink of course, but serving him anything he enjoys (pipe, whiskey, rack-of-lamb...) after a stressful day will make him feel like a king.

32

If a man cannot trust you, he cannot open up his heart to you.

Don't give a man any reason to think that he cannot trust you. In a relationship, absolute loyalty to the man you love will help him to open up to you. Emotional intimacy for a lot of guys is risky business. If you earn his trust ensure that you don't do anything to lose it.

33

He doesn't mind it if you help him to lead.

If you want a man to take the lead in a certain situation, tell him that you want him to make the decision because you trust his judgment. A man likes being told how great his decision-making ability is. Learn how to feed his manly ego and encourage him to make better decisions more consistently.

34

Men love women that communicate with class.

It's not what you say to him that matters the most, but how you say it. If you want a man to respond favorably towards you, communicate with class. Nagging works in a negative way. He'll resent your nagging and will avoid it at all cost (sometimes by avoiding the truth). You can be angry, upset, frustrated, and even disappointed, but always, always...be respectful.

35

We secretly wish we were more romantic,

more often. It just feels...awkward.

Some men don't like being romantic because it just feels uncomfortable. Others feel as if their romantic efforts won't make much of a difference. Be sure that you show him that they do. Don't gloss over the little things because he neglects the major, and vice versa. If he's not naturally romantic then be patient with him. It even helps to tell him what you like and even how you'd like to be treated.

36

There's something about you he never

wants to change.

He first fell in love with you because of _____. Whatever you fill in that blank with, if possible, NEVER change that thing. There's always something about the woman we fell in love with that we don't want to change. Sometimes it's a physical feature, but for most guys it's a certain personality trait or quality. A good man will love you unconditionally, but why make loving you a challenge? If there's something about you that he fell in love with, and it's within your power to keep, don't change it.

37

He wants you to at least make a courtesy reach.

Contrary to popular belief, it is not a rule that a man should pay for you *if you both agreed* to meet for a dinner date. However, if the gentleman is willing, it would benefit you to at least have the courtesy to reach for the bill. Let him insist on paying if he so chooses, but do not presume that he should pay your way, especially if there has been no establishment of a romantic relationship.

38

Men need some downtime immediately after work.

When he gets home after work, resist the temptation to inundate him with all the happenings of your day or your misadventures. Help him relax by keeping the conversation light unless he suggests otherwise. Give him the opportunity to settle down and quiet his mind, especially if he has a stressful job.

39

He wants you to be sexy a little more often.

A little fixing up to impress your man seldom goes unnoticed. Consistently going the extra mile to make yourself sexually appealing to your man can do wonders to pique his interest in you. Sometimes your body language is the only thing you need to convince a man.

40

If your man works hard to provide for you, you should likewise work hard to keep him.

Don't get lazy. Many women fall prey to the idea that once they have a man keeping him is easy as pie. These women soon wake up one day to realize how wrong they were! If your man works exceedingly hard to provide for you in any capacity, ensure that you learn him in and out so that you can keep him happy. Never take him for granted, as there are probably a ton of women out there with their eyes on what you fail to appreciate.

41

If he tells you "no", respect his decision.

If your man tells you "no", and he feels strongly about it, respect his decision. Even if you think he's wrong, respect his decision. Even if you want to bring the issue up again, do so in a respectful way. You don't have to agree with him or even follow his orders if they're completely nonsensical, but at least show him that you respectfully disagree.

42

We can be trained to treat you like a lady.
But ensure that you act like one first.

Some men aren't as refined as others. If you want a man to be a gentleman, act like a lady. Men naturally love to protect that which is beautiful and delicate. Class, feminine gracefulness, and modesty are the keys to unlocking a man's desire to dote.

43

Don't let the kids dictate your sex life.

Your mileage may vary with this one depending on the age of your children, but when they're able to understand, teach your children to respect mommy and daddy's alone time. They should not dictate this area of your life. No man wants to feel as if he has to beg and cajole his wife for some alone time away from the kids. Show an interest in pleasing him sexually and ensure that your sex life maintains its vigor even after the kids arrive.

Chapter 4:

Don't - How to Make Him Lose Interest in You

44

No man wants to be your project. Don't make him feel that way by trying to change him.

The more you try to force a man to change the more he will resist you. And even if you do get him to change, chances are it will be temporary and he will feel resentful towards you. A man doesn't mind being graciously *influenced* by the woman he loves, but no man in his *right mind* wants a woman to make him over. It's better to find a man who's already committed to constantly improving himself than it is to find one you need to "mold" into the man you want him to be.

45

Men don't enjoy girl talk.

We don't. No sensible man does, so don't try to have "girl talk" with us. "Girl talk" is reserved for girls not guys, girls. That's you, your sisters, your mother, your girlfriends, and even your cat, Bessie. Do not try to get a man to have "girl talk" with you.

46

News flash: We don't want to "complete" you.

No man can complete you. He can only complement you. So don't go into a relationship expecting him to fill in your missing pieces. And though you've probably heard this all before, I'll repeat it again...high self-esteem is attractive in a woman. Loving and respecting yourself makes you far more attractive to a man.

47

Most men don't enjoy shopping. He will tolerate it to make you happy.

In all honesty, you do have some guys out there that LOVE to go shopping with their wives or girlfriends. These are the select few. For most men however, shopping with their significant other is nowhere near as much fun as NOT shopping with their significant other. Yes, we know it makes you happy and all warm-inside to be out in public with a man of your own. So if you must invite us to shop, at least find a way to make it worth our while.

48

Nagging is the ultimate turn off. If you want something done, try a different tactic.

If you want to get a man to do something grudgingly and with a lot of resentment, nag him to do it. If you want to get a man to do something willingly and with a good attitude, try a little tenderness instead. Imagine you were royalty and you wanted to persuade the heads-of-state to follow your advice or to do something that they found disagreeable. How would you coerce such powerful men to take action without disrespecting them or losing their adoration for you? Persuasive lips make a woman irresistible to the man that loves her.

49

Never ask your family for financial help before consulting with your husband.

Unless your husband has a serious spending problem (or some other financially debilitating issue), when it comes to money always keep your husband in the loop. Even if your mother or sister needs a small loan from you, don't give in to their demands without talking things out with your husband. Full disclosure is essential when it comes to financial matters in a marriage.

50

Do not make a habit of exalting other men.

No matter how close you are with your co-worker, boss, etc., excessively referring to what another man says and does is intolerable. No man wants to feel as if you respect or admire another man more than you do him. And never, ever compare your husband or boyfriend with someone else's. Habitually exalting or comparing your husband or boyfriend to other men is a sure recipe for disaster.

51

Never insult or belittle a man in front of his children. Never.

Having the respect and admiration of our offspring is vitally important to us as men. If you would have words with him, do so in private and away from your/his children. Do not allow a young lady or a young man to witness you disrespecting their father (figure of authority). It will have a negative impact on your relationship as well as their development.

52

We want you to be authentically attractive.

Never try to change yourself to attract a man. Your unique quirks and qualities will always be attractive to the guy who's right for you. The more you try to change yourself to fit his particular interests the more resentment you'll feel for both him and yourself. The right man will love your natural personality; he will adore your integrity as a woman.

53

A smart man will avoid a miserable woman like the plague.

Nothing turns a man off faster than a miserable woman. The only man who wants a miserable woman is a miserable man...or a man nobody else wants. Keep that in mind.

54

Never belittle, insult, or harshly tease a man in front of his friends.

Insulting or deriding a man in front of others shows disrespect, and unless it's fun, harmless jesting...he will resent it. Of course, if you both have the quirky kind of relationship where you enjoy having it out in front of friends, by all means go at it. But I doubt this is the case. No man likes being derided by his woman (or any woman) in front of his close friends and associates (or even strangers for that matter).

55

Try to be a little less ambiguous with your moods.

No man wants to play "guess what I'm upset about right now?" with his woman. If a man asks you what's wrong, tell him. The more you hem and haw around the issue, the more stress and anxiety you'll put on him.

Don't play emotional games with a man who's genuinely concerned about your welfare.

56

In a serious commitment, a man doesn't want to compete with your friends.

Don't make a man compete with your friends if he's genuinely interested in forming a long-term commitment with you. Don't make him feel as if he'll always be playing second-fiddle to your girlfriends. Yes, your friends are very important to you, but are they hindering or helping you to find and keep the man of your dreams? Some women make the mistake of placing "sisterhood" above the happiness of their significant other. If you're very close to the women in your life, find a way to bring more cohesion to your dating and social life. Unless you have man-hating, argumentative girlfriends, if he's genuinely interested in being with you he'll be genuinely interested in befriending your friends as well.

57

Men HATE being manipulated and watching other men being manipulated.

A good man will not tolerate being manipulated. No matter how attractive you think you are, if he thinks you're just interested in getting your way at his expense, he WILL abandon you. This sentiment is universal. No man in his *right mind* desires to be manipulated by a woman.

58

He will trust you only as much as he trusts the company you keep.

If a man senses that you value the opinions of your perpetually single, man-bashing friends more than his, you'll slowly lose his trust and adoration. Why are you friends with perpetually single, man-bashing women in the first place? During your first encounters with him, a man will often make judgments about you based on the friends you keep.

59

Flirting with guys is no longer appropriate after you've committed to someone.

Your mileage may vary on this one depending on the guy you're dating (or in a serious relationship with), but from my experience and observations, no man wants to be in a serious relationship with a woman who insists on flirting with other men. It's not flattering and it is downright disrespectful. And if you're really serious about making your relationship last, it can be downright dangerous.

60

Most men keep female best friends that they find attractive in some way.

Men and women cannot truly be best friends without there being some form of attraction. I say this because even though the woman may be thinking they're just friends, the guy may still see her as an "option" someday. This one might be difficult to swallow, but in a lot of cases there's the potential for some form of sexual chemistry. I'm not saying that all male-female friendships have a sexual component to it, but there is a high possibility that someone will eventually feel sexual tension, whether they want to admit it or not.

61

Self-pity is undesirable in a woman, especially when she's comparing herself to other women.

It sounds harsh, but I like to tell it like it is...self-pity isn't sexy on a woman. Okay, in all honesty, self-pity isn't attractive for men either, but when a woman tells her man that she thinks her girlfriends and/or co-workers are *more attractive* or *more desirable* than her, she's playing a dangerous game. No man wants to think that maybe he should have dated your *more attractive* girlfriend. And he doesn't want to entertain the idea that dating your *more desirable* co-worker would have been way more rewarding.

Even if you feel low, never negate your own strengths and beauty while communicating with your man. He can only do so much to encourage you, but his confidence in you is directly link to your own self-confidence. Don't give him any reason to think that he chose poorly.

49

62

Don't date his friends, especially if you secretly harbor fantasies of someday reuniting.

If you date any of his friends after you've dated him, forget about trying to get him back in the future. For most guys, once you've cross that line...you're dead to him. This isn't a hard and fast rule but it's something that you should keep in mind if you think you might want to get back together with an ex-boyfriend. I repeat, don't date his friends if you see future potential in him.

63

If you're dating a man who starts to pull away from you, don't "reward" him with more love and attention.

Men don't usually view the world in terms of relationships; they view the world in terms of successes and failures. Therefore, we act either to avoid losing something or in the hope of gaining something. If a man is losing interest in you (pulling away), showering him with more love and attention will only hasten his emotional retreat.

Chasing a retreating man makes you even less desirable because he'll know for a fact that he "has you" and can act as he pleases simply because the value you've placed on him is much higher than the value he's placed on you. Instead of caving in, the smart woman will busy herself with her own interests and seek the company of those who value her companionship. If he's for real, he will come back to his senses and do what he can to regain your favor. Some men really, really want the space (and motivation) to pursue a woman.

64

Do not insult his mother.

I repeat: Do not insult a man's mother. No matter how controlling, domineering, irrational, unreasonable, or intolerable you think she is, do not insult his mother. Obviously having a mother like this is enough grief for him, and he probably already knows that you two don't get along well. Don't make it more difficult for him by bad-mouthing her every chance you get. She might be a crazy witch, but she still breast-fed the man you love.

65

**It causes a man grief when you habitually
look messy and unkempt.**

This one may be tough to swallow for some women
but it still needs to be said. Men love looking at beautiful
things, and your man desperately wants the most
beautiful thing he's ever seen to be you. Of course, no
woman will always be on her "A" game, and no woman
should ever be forced to be on display all the time.

However, the ugly truth is that men are far more
judgmental towards a woman's appearance than women
are towards men. Stringy hair, sweaty armpits, unshaved
legs, and tattered clothing won't win you any awards.
Looking bad shows a man that you don't care much
about yourself and that you care even less about having
a man. Keep that in mind.

66

Men hate being interrupted.

I've heard this complaint from other men quite often,
and I've experienced it as well. When a woman

interrupts you mid-sentence, consistently, it is not only annoying...it can be infuriating. Once again, it's a minor sign of disrespect and a lack of tact to interrupt someone mid-sentence. Women are often quicker of thought, and some feel the need to say something as soon as it enters their mind. This might not annoy every man, but you'd be surprised how many men find this sort of communication frustrating. Let the man talk. If you don't let him speak his mind the way he wants...prepare for a very, very silent relationship.

67

Don't make him dote on you unnecessarily.

It's emasculating to hold your handbags. It's annoying to have to wait on you while you talk to your girlfriends in the mall. It's not fun always having "honey-do's." And it's definitely unflattering if he's always buying your beauty and feminine products.

Don't always insist that a man *should* do these things because he loves you. He doesn't mind doing them from time to time, but don't turn it into his full-time (or even part-time) job. Don't make him dote on you unnecessarily. His chivalry will soon turn dead.

68

If you can't hold your liquor, don't drink.

When choosing a long-term mate for a life of love, men look for both beauty AND <u>virtue</u> in a woman. Thus, when it comes to alcohol, a woman who drinks and carouses without limitation is particularly unattractive to high-quality men. Such behavior screams poor character and bad decision-making, and sagacious men know that ending up with such a woman could jeopardize their future happiness. High-quality men tend to appraise the people, places, and things around them. Hence, in their eyes, a woman who drinks and carouses without restraint is a high risk, and thus undesirable for a serious relationship. It's the ugly truth.

69

Don't play dumb.

No good man who has his head screwed on properly is going to date or cultivate a relationship with a woman who enjoys playing the role of bimbo. If you consciously choose to be an airhead, you'll attract men who value airheads. Men of substance enjoy being around women of substance. Playing dumb to get a man's attention is immature. No sensible man is expecting you to be a Harvard graduate, he only expects you to have both competency and integrity.

Chapter 5:

Sex, Passion, And Intimacy

70

Handjobs are very much welcomed.

Learning how to give a handjob is a masterful skill that some husbands wish their wives knew. I'm sure you can imagine that those wives who know how to give masterful handjobs have very, very happy husbands. If you can pleasure your husband to the point that he melts in your hands, you'll be surprised at just how affectionate he can be.

And the best part about this technique is that you can get creative about where and when you do it. It's perfect for giving him those quickie pleasures when he starts getting frisky with you in the most random of places. Besides, it's a great skill to learn especially if you're uncomfortable performing oral sex on him.

71

Give your husband oral sex, regardless.

If your husband wants oral sex and you don't want to give it to him because you're not confident about it, get over it. For men, bad oral sex is like bad pizza. You'd have to try REALLY hard to mess it up. Men usually want it regardless.

72

Sex is a great stress reliever after a long day.

Scx releases endorphins that make us feel good, and it's a great tension reliever. If your husband has a very stressful job, chances are he's going to need a lot of time to unwind when he gets home. Surprise him every now and then with some spontaneous sex as he settles in from a long day's work.

73

Men love it when their wives initiate sex.

Having a sexually assertive wife is a desire that many men possess. So when the woman we love takes the initiative in getting her sexual needs met, it makes us feel desirable and boosts our self-esteem. Because one of the ways a man will show his love is through physical intimacy, i.e. sex, having his wife take the initiative from time to time lets him know that she still finds him irresistibly attractive. Don't be shy or think that his opinion of you will change for the worse if you become a little more sexually assertive. He probably wants you to be.

74

We want to see you in sexy lingerie...as often as we can.

Lingerie can work wonders on a man's imagination, provided it's the kind of lingerie *he* enjoys seeing you in. Variety is the spice of wife. So spice things up with your husband by growing your collection of sexy lingerie. While it's good to surprise him from time to time, make sure that you get his input as well so that you know exactly what will turn him on the most.

Your husband might care less if you paraded around in a baby doll, but he might drool all over the carpet if you stride around in fishnets. Don't be offended if he doesn't respond to certain types. Keep experimenting until you find something enjoyable for you both.

75

A man uses all five of his senses to determine attraction. So smell appealing.

As men, we may be driven by what we see with our eyes, but what we smell also plays a huge part in the game of attraction. To this day I can still remember the names of women that had the habit of making themselves smell tantalizingly good. So believe me, investing in body oils, perfumes, etc. that work well with your natural scent can increase your desirability to a man.

76

Penis size isn't everything. Seriously!

Here's an interesting scientific fact: The length of a flaccid penis does not necessarily suggest its erected length. The average erect length is about 5-6 inches. In short, there's no guarantee that a man with a big penis is going to be able to satisfy you any more than a man with an average sized one. Besides, most of a woman's vaginal sensitivity is in the front of her vagina, but I'm sure you already knew that.

77

When a man is interested in you, he'll quickly categorize you as either a short-term conquest or a long-term companion.

Men are driven to procreate and please themselves. If you want a man to perceive you as more than just an object for procreation and pleasure, don't let him think that you're a slut. Having sex with a lot of different men might make a woman feel "liberated" or "modern", but to most guys, she's just a good time. Even to guys who are looking for a long-term commitment, she's just a way to pass the time. Nothing more.

78

We want you all to ourselves, even before we met you.

Deep down, all men wish for their wives to be virgins. If he loves you, he wouldn't wish to have shared you with anyone else. This doesn't mean that he'll resent your past or even make a fuss about it, but at some point the thought probably crossed his mind.

79

When it comes to vaginas, cleanliness equals sexiness.

Not every man wants or needs a shaved vagina, but every man wants a very clean one. How a woman smells down there can make a big difference when it comes to sexual intimacy. An odorless vagina is a healthy vagina and it tells a man that you take excellent care of yourself. Even the tightness of a vagina makes a difference to a man. The tighter it is the more pleasure a man derives from sexual intercourse. The more pleasure he feels, the more addicted to you he becomes.

80

If he isn't satisfying you sexually, be kind in letting him know.

No man wants to hear that he's an inefficient lover in bed. But if you must tell him you're unsatisfied, do so with class and gentleness. This can be a very sensitive subject, but in a loving marriage it's important to communicate with honesty. And don't tell him he's not doing it right while you're in bed. Wait for another time to have that talk. Don't allow him to associate the bedroom with your sexual dissatisfaction.

Chapter 6:

On Finding Mr. Right

81

If you want to date a manly man, then be more feminine.

It's quite true that polar opposites (masculine and feminine) attract each other like magnets. Men who relish the fact that they are MEN are helplessly drawn to women who deeply appreciate their womanhood. If you prefer being with a more masculine man then enhance your own femininity. Your feminine grace, modesty, passion, and joie de vivre are all inner qualities that strong, masculine men find irresistible in a woman.

82

Marriage is a HUGE deal for a man, and he makes his decision when both his heart and his brain are in agreement.

For many men, the decision to marry requires more than just love; it actually has to make logical sense to him. He needs both his heart and his brain to be in agreement about you before he can take things to the next level. For some men, marriage can be like a business decision, a life investment. If a man thinks he'll lose too much by committing his life to a woman…she's screwed.

83

It's just as important to look for the right relationship as well as the right man.

The right man will give you the commitment that you're really looking for. Falling in love with a man who's not ready to give you the kind of commitment you deserve will only make things difficult for both you and him, especially you. You can actually find a really decent guy who has the qualities of your Mr. Right, but if his heart isn't ready to commit to you, you're out of luck.

Don't try to force a round peg into a square hole. Wait for Mr. Right who also wants the right kind of commitment. Sometimes a man won't commit because the time isn't right for him. In such cases, it may be better to move on and wait for something a little better to come along.

84

Submissive body language is far more attractive to a man who wants a relationship.

If you want men to approach you, don't make a habit of making yourself *look* unapproachable. If you try to look unapproachable to scare off the guys you don't want you may also end up scaring off the guys you are attracted to. Your body language may be subtle, but men can pick up on whether or not a woman is approachable. Learn how to make your body language more attractive and friendly. Men find warm, feminine body language sexy when they're looking for a potential partner.

85

If a man shows interest in you, refrain from trying to make him feel as if he's "The One" right away. You might lose both him and your sanity.

It doesn't matter how "dreamy" you think he is. If you make a man your "world" before he even gets a chance to know you, you're going to scare him off. Try to rein in your emotions and give him time to chase and pursue you. Give him a fair challenge and slowly seduce him with your feminine charms. Trust me, men love a challenge; so don't make a man your world as soon as he shows an interest in you. A busy woman is a desirable woman. He will want to work for your attention. So don't let him think you're starved for male attention, even if you are!

86

Yes, it's okay to flirt with a man you're interested in. In fact, it's encouraged. We want you to make it happen.

It's quite an ego booster for a man when a woman goes out of her way to flirt with him. It's okay to initiate flirting with a guy you find attractive or interesting. If he's a classy kind of guy, he'll flirt with you as well, unless he's already taken. And if he's genuinely not interested, that's okay; he'll be a gentleman about it, I can guarantee you. So long as you can do it in a coquettish and come-hither way, don't be afraid to hit on that guy you find a little "dreamy." Most guys want women to be a little more flirtatious with them anyway. The rewards always go to the bold.

87

Be an interesting person. Interesting men enjoy being around interesting women.

You can lose a man's interest in you simply by being boring. I've met boring women and have even dated one or two (for an extremely short amount of time). They just weren't that interesting, but being young and full of hormones I overlooked this observation at the time because I found them physically attractive. Physical beauty can only get you so far with men, but if you want your interactions with men to be much more substantial, become an interesting woman.

Your friends, hobbies, dreams, and aspirations all add up to make you an interesting person. If you find that guys only enjoy your company when you're being physical with them, you probably need to be a little more interesting (and perhaps even a little more discriminating with the men you date). Develop your interests so that you can attract more substantial relationships with guys who not only find you attractive, but intriguing as well.

88

Carefully observe the way a man treats his mother because that is the level of respect he is most likely going to show you.

How we treat our mothers is a mirror to how we may treat you now or in the future. Find a man who believes that mothers should be treated with respect, honor, and kindness. Of course, I'm not saying to go out and find a mama's boy who wants to do anything to please his mother. What I am saying is to find a man who respects his mother and treats her with compassion, but who also knows how to set boundaries with her in order to maintain an ADULT relationship. You'll save yourself a lot of headache by avoiding men who either treat their mothers poorly or who treat them like goddesses.

89

Studying a man's friends, close co-workers, and heroes will give you a lot of

insight into what influences his beliefs and behavior.

Ladies, here's the big secret to understanding a man: Observe his social circles and his sources of inspiration. Ask him about his friends and closest co-workers and even try to spend some time getting to know them. Watch his favorite movies with him and observe how he reacts. Ask him about his favorite books and what inspires him. The benefit to this is two-fold.

First, you'll learn a GREAT deal about what makes him tick as a man and you'll be better able to understand what drives his behavior. The second thing is that the more interested in him you become the more emotionally connected he'll *feel* towards you. He'll feel as if you "get him" and he'll feel compelled to spend as much time with you as he humanly can.

Chapter 7:

What A Good Man Prefers

90

We love smart women; we just don't want constant displays of "obnoxious intelligence" flung in our face all the time.

This is the other side of the "don't play dumb" coin. Some women enjoy forcing their intellect on others, especially men. This is only problematic when the man you're interested in has no interest in competing with you intellectually. Notice, I didn't say that he doesn't want an intellectual EQUAL or even a woman who may naturally be much smarter than he is.

All I'm saying is that he doesn't want to compete with the intellect of his feminine companion by having to deal with a "know-it-all" attitude. I'm sure you can agree that it's equally annoying as a woman to deal with a man who insists on flaunting his storehouse of knowledge. A man prefers to *discover* the depth of a woman's intellect over time and on his own as opposed to having all of her learning thrown in his face at every opportunity.

91

Men pay special attention to how you treat other men, especially when you treat other men like dirt.

A wise man will watch how you treat your good old Dad, brothers, or male friends to judge how you'll treat him in the future. If he sees you treating the men in your life like scum, he's going to run for his life! So don't go around man-bashing, criticizing the men in your life, or constantly complaining about how your Dad is so useless or how your co-worker Mike is so lazy, or how your ex-boyfriend didn't buy you enough stuff. Every complaint and bad behavior towards men, especially the men you have or *had* relationships with, is being recorded somewhere in the back of his brain.

92

Most men would love for you to stay home and raise a family if they could afford it.

A lot of guys out there still maintain a traditional

view of how a home is made and how a family is raised. Due to the economic times it seems to be a little more difficult for men to be the sole breadwinner while a woman maintains the home and creates a wonderful nest for the family to grow. But the economic climate doesn't change a man's desire to provide for those he loves and have a supportive wife who can handle the management of the home. There are many guys out there who would still prefer to have their wives be homemakers than to be out in the workplace, if only they could earn enough money to do so sustainably.

93

A word about men and ultimatums...

Giving a man an ultimatum won't win you any popularity awards with him. In fact, it might be just the opposite. Whenever you give him an ultimatum, just know that there is a chance of him resenting you for it. Also, if you give a man an ultimatum, expect the best but be prepared for the worst. And if you absolutely must give a man an ultimatum concerning your relationship, ensure that you trust his ability to make the right decision for the both of you.

94

Most men actually prefer your natural beauty. Try that on sometimes.

There's nothing wrong with a little make up every now and then, but if there's one complaint I hear from a lot of guys is that the women they know wear far too much makeup too much of the time. What's funny about this is that some men prefer a woman who uses makeup modestly if at all. There's something irresistible about a woman who knows how to illustrate her best features through natural beautification. Ladies, sometimes less is more. Let a man appreciate the real you.

95

An angry man requires space and time to regain his composure.

You WILL test his patience, make him angry, and push all of his buttons from time to time. Give him some time to cool off before you interact with him. Don't add fuel to the fire by getting all up in his face and being a general nuisance. If he leaves an argument so that he can cool off, do not follow him. Allow him to return to you. A good man will return once he's regained his composure.

96

You're way more attractive when you dress very feminine.

Tight jeans and a T-shirt can be sexy, but they're still no match for nicely shaved legs and a pretty skirt or dress. Men are helplessly drawn to women who embrace all aspects of their femininity, especially the way a woman dresses herself. You can wear pants and put your hair in a cute little bun all you want, but what may really get his attention are some pumps, some hanging earrings, and a sexy, form-fitting (yet classy) dress.

97

Gentleness in a woman is highly sought after by men, especially high-quality men.

Men crave for the gentleness of women (but would rarely admit it), especially in today's modern society where women are just as competitive and aggressive as men. Men often find the "modern" woman to be far too competitive, indifferent, and combative for their tastes, and yet they try to deal with it as best as they can. Most men would prefer to have a woman who is more loving, cooperative, and supportive; a suitable partner. Men have enough competition, indifference, and aggression to deal with in their work and social relations with each other; don't be another source of pain and conflict for him.

98

Believe it or not, guys have feelings too.

Yes, men have emotions. Some men are better at expressing them than others, but that doesn't negate the fact that men do have feelings. It's easier for a woman to hurt a man's feelings than another man. That's the kind of power you have with a man. Just be aware that misuse of your influence over him will result in you losing his adoration and love. Be careful what you say to him and about him. And although we won't always ask for it...we want you to apologize when you *know* you should.

99

On the quest to find the perfect girl, men love an exciting, but fair challenge.

Here's the ugly truth: If you make anything too easy for a man, especially an ambitious man, you're setting yourself up for a disappointing relationship. High-status, high-quality, ambitious men are goal-driven and love having to work towards something. If you give him your full time and attention too quickly, he'll have nothing to aim for. He'll feel cheated out of the chase and will choose to look elsewhere for sport. Sadly, the poor chap loses interest in you not because he didn't want you, but because you didn't make him believe you were worth pursuing.

100

If you can't pay him your undivided attention, he won't enjoy spending quality time with you.

When a man is giving you his full, undivided

attention and you're unable to reciprocate, in the least it will irritate him. Not being able to maintain eye contact, fidgeting, checking your phone, butting in with a random observation, etc. is not endearing, it's rude. If a man is really speaking his mind and trying to connect with you, give him your undivided attention and resolute focus. Quiet your mind and *really* listen to what he's trying to communicate. If your man likes to talk, he will fall in love with the woman who lets him. You've been warned.

101

We'd prefer to be ignorant of your beautification paraphernalia.

You can use just about whatever you want to work your beauty magic, just don't let us see what's behind the curtain. Translation: Most men don't want to deal with a messy trail of cosmetic products, dirty underwear, and other feminine items in their homes (or yours for that matter). We're only interested in the end result, so try to keep the magic recipe to yourself and out of sight. We'll greatly appreciate this, thanks.

Final Thoughts

Whether you want to attract the man of your dreams, make your boyfriend or husband happy, or get him to open up emotionally, you must understand how he thinks and what his deepest needs are. Only by understanding a man will you be able to connect with him like no other woman can. And it's this emotional connection with you that can make him fall and stay in love with you.

Your *feminine influence* over a man is the key to his heart, and you can only influence that which you understand. Men WANT to be influenced by the woman they love and adore. We WANT to be seduced and catered to and treated like kings from the one woman we can't resist. We crave it, albeit secretly, and like I said before, we'll give our hearts and the world to a woman that just "gets us."

Have you ever wondered why some women can get a man to commit and some cannot? Or have you ever been puzzled as to why some women enjoy blissful, romantic relationships with amazing men who just want to make them happy? Well, more than likely these women understand the power that they have over men. And more importantly, they use this power to HEAL, NURTURE, and positively INFLUENCE the man that they love.

This is something that all men need and secretly want from the woman they love. But as I mentioned in the

83

introduction, most guys either don't know that in order to fully love a woman they must open their hearts to them or even if they do know, they don't know how to do it. But you as a woman are in a very unique position. The way you communicate with a man through your words and actions, no matter how subtle, will be the determining factor in whether or not he connects with you emotionally and opens up his heart to you.

Why is it so important for a man to open up his heart to you? Well, in order for him to DECIDE to commit to you, he's going to have to feel as if a life without you just doesn't make logical sense. And before he can love you with all that he has he needs to feel that deep connection. He's going to need a deep feeling of emotional security with you, knowing that whether he's up or down, weak or strong, stoic or emotional, that you'll always be there for him and that you'll never PERCEIVE him as weak and vulnerable.

Read that last paragraph again before you read on...

Men love to be seen as strong and capable of handling anything that comes their way. So when things don't work out as they should or when they experience moments of powerlessness, they need the support of a woman who can heal the hurt, nurture the pain, and encourage them when they need it most. Are you the kind of woman that a man can fully trust with his emotions, or are does your attitude hold him back from giving you full access to his heart?

Give it some thought, and if you feel as if your own interactions with men could use some improvement, begin to develop a more graceful, nurturing nature. Learn what feminine gracefulness is and how to become an irresistible woman that men adore. Because without feminine gracefulness, even if you are able to attract and keep a man in your life, chances are you won't be able to get him to open up emotionally. You may find yourself having trouble getting him to commit to you all the way, or even worse, he may never be "all there" with you emotionally. And this is something that no woman wants to end up with.

By the way...

As a way of saying "thanks" for your purchase, I'm offering a free 10-lesson email course (and other assorted goodies) that are exclusive to my book readers. Each lesson reveals some of my best-kept dating secrets for cultivating long-term attraction with high-quality men.

You can access it at:

http://www.brucebryans.com/ecourse/

In this free course you will learn the most attractive dating habits of high-value women; the kind of women that make men burn with desire and desperate to commit to them. You will also discover the secrets to having more confidence and power with men and dating so that you can get the guy you want, keep him interested, and quickly weed out the time-wasters, the players, and the men who'll never commit.

In this knowledge-packed course, you'll discover:

- How to stand your ground and confidently communicate your boundaries in a way that INCREASES a man's attraction to you instead of turning him off.

- The one thing you absolutely MUST do when the man you love and want begins to pull away from you in a relationship.

- How to quickly hook Mr. Right from the first few dates by doing something MOST women are terrified of doing after meeting a great guy.

- What to do when a man says he "loves you" but he doesn't call you enough (or perhaps even at all).

- The #1 key to conquering the masculine heart and how to use this knowledge to cultivate DEEP feelings of love in a man. (Hint: This is the fastest way to tap into a man's emotional needs and make him see you as "Girlfriend Material.")

- A simple way to SKYROCKET your chances of meeting Mr. Right instead of desperately waiting for a "stroke of luck" to change your love life.

- And much, much more…

Enter the web address below into your Internet browser and join the thousands of other women who have used these attraction secrets to get more confidence, power, and results with men and dating.

Again, you can access it at:

http://www.brucebryans.com/ecourse/

See you on the inside,

Bruce

Before you go...

I just wanted to say "thank you" for purchasing my book.

I know you could have picked from dozens of books on understanding men, but you took a chance on my guide and for that I'm extremely grateful. So, thanks again for purchasing this book and reading all the way to the end.

Now, if you liked this book, **please take a minute or two to leave a review for it on Amazon so that other women just like you can find out more about it**. Your feedback is most appreciated as it helps me to continue writing books that get you results.

And "thank you" in advance for your review. I am eternally grateful.

Dating & Attraction Books by Bruce Bryans:

Below is a list of my books for women that you can find on Amazon.com. You can easily find them all here at: http://www.amazon.com/author/brucebryans

***

Texts So Good He Can't Ignore: Sassy Texting Secrets for Attracting High-Quality Men (and Keeping the One You Want)

In *Texts So Good He Can't Ignore*, you'll discover how to use texting to easily create attraction with your guy and finally get him OFF of his smartphone and ON more dates with you.

Never Chase Men Again: 38 Dating Secrets to Get the Guy, Keep Him Interested, and Avoid Dead-End Relationships

In *Never Chase Men Again*, you'll learn how to get the guy you want, train him to pursue you, and avoid dead-end or even "dead-on-arrival" relationships by being more assertive and communicating high-value to the men you date.

How To Get A Man Without Getting Played: 29 Dating Secrets to Catch Mr. Right, Set Your Standards, and Eliminate Time Wasters

In *How To Get A Man Without Getting Played*, you'll discover the beliefs, attitudes, dating rules, "love habits", and seduction secrets high-value women use to eliminate time wasters and find Mr. Right.

He's Not That Interested, He's Just Passing Time: 40 Unmistakable Behaviors of Men Who Avoid Commitment and Play Games with Women

In *He's Not That Interested, He's Just Passing Time*, you'll learn how to read a man's behavior to find out if he wants a relationship with you or if he's just leading you on and completely wasting your time.

Keep Calm And Cut Him Off: 13 Reasons to "Go Silent" on Guys Who Reject or Break Up with You

In *Keep Calm And Cut Him Off*, you'll learn the importance of silence after a guy loses interest, and how to use it to reclaim your power after a breakup or quickly bounce back from male rejection.

Never Get Ghosted Again: 15 Reasons Why Men Lose Interest and How to Avoid Guys Who Can't Commit

In *Never Get Ghosted Again*, you'll discover the secret reasons why men lose interest, what causes men to fall in and out of love, and how to prevent great guys from disappearing on you.

The 7 Irresistible Qualities Men Want In A Woman: What High-Quality Men Secretly Look for When Choosing "The One"

In *The 7 Irresistible Qualities Men Want In A Woman*, you'll discover the feminine qualities that commitment ready, high-quality men look for when choosing a long-term mate.

Make Him BEG For Your Attention: 75 Communication Secrets for Captivating Men and Getting the Love and Commitment You Deserve

In *Make Him BEG For Your Attention*, you'll discover how to talk to a man so that he listens to you, opens up to you, and gives you what you want without a fuss.

Dating Deal Breakers That Drive Men Away: 12 Relationship Killers That Ruin Your Long-term Potential with High-Quality Men

In *Dating Deal Breakers That Drive Men Away*, you'll learn the most common dating red flags that high-quality men consider "deal-breakers", the kind of deal-breakers that compel them to stop pursuing a woman, ignore her texts (and phone calls), and eventually blow up a budding relationship.

Send Him A Signal: 61 Secrets for Indicating Interest and Attracting the Attention of Higher Quality Men

In *Send Him A Signal*, you'll learn the subtle signs of female interest that entices men to pursue a woman and also how to become more approachable to high-quality guys.

101 Things Your Dad Never Told You About Men: The Good, Bad, and Ugly Things Men Want and Think About Women and Relationships

In *101 Things Your Dad Never Told You About Men*, you'll learn what high-quality men want from women and what they think about love, sex, and romance. You'll learn how to seduce the man you want or captivate the man you love because you'll know exactly what makes him tick.

101 Reasons Why He Won't Commit To You: The Secret Fears, Doubts, and Insecurities That Prevent Most Men from Getting Married

In *101 Reasons Why He Won't Commit To You*, you'll learn the most common fears, doubts, and insecurities that paralyze men and prevent them from making the leap from boyfriend to husband.

About Bruce Bryans

Bruce Bryans is a successful author with a passion for research into the dating and mating rituals of men and women. He doesn't fashion himself as some all-knowing "relationship guru", but instead prefers to provide insightful information based on the social and biological factors that bring men and women together for love and romance. Bruce has written numerous books on topics including: masculinity, attraction, dating strategy, and gender dynamics within romantic relationships. Bruce's main aim is to provide easy-to-implement, practical information that helps men and women improve their dating market value and mating desirability to the opposite sex.

When he isn't tucked away in some corner writing a literary masterpiece (or so he thinks), Bruce spends most of his time engaged in manly hobbies, spending time with friends, or being a lovable nuisance to his wife and children.

You can learn more about his writings and receive updates (and future discounts) on his books by visiting his website at: www.BruceBryans.com

Share the Secrets

If you've been empowered, enlightened, or helped in any way by this book, please recommend it to your sisters, daughters, co-workers, and friends. If you're a blogger or fellow author, consider recommending it to your readers. And if you're a dating coach, therapist, counselor, etc., and you strongly believe that this book can help your clients, please consider recommending it to them or purchasing copies to give away as gifts.

I sincerely hope this book does wonders not only for your love life, but for the lives of the women you care about as well.

Here's to your success!

Bruce Bryans

Made in the USA
Las Vegas, NV
12 March 2025

19463440R00059